Communi
Activities
with Adults

CW00933057

Communication
Activities
with Adults

Jayne Comins
Felicity Llewellyn
& Judith Offiler

Speechmark Publishing Ltd
Telford Road • Bicester • Oxon • OX26 4LQ • United Kingdom

Special thanks to Phil Goddard and Peter and Jolene Comins

Published by
Speechmark Publishing Ltd, Telford Road, Bicester, Oxon OX26 4LQ,
United Kingdom
Tel: +44 (0)1869 244 644   Fax: +44 (0)1869 320 040
www.speechmark.net

002-5098/Printed in the United Kingdom/1010

British Library Cataloguing in Publication Data
Comins, Jayne
    Communication activities with adults. – Rev. ed. – (A Speechmark creative
    groupwork resource)
    1. Speech therapy – Exercises 2. Language disorders – Treatment 3. Old age
    homes – Activity programs 4. Adult day care centers – Activity programs
    I. Title II. Llewellyn, Felicity III. Offiler, Judy IV. Comins, Jayne. Activites and ideas
    616.8'55'06515

ISBN-10: 0 86388 343 5
ISBN-13: 978 0 86388 343 9

CONTENTS

Introduction xi

About the Authors xiii

CUED RESPONSES

1 Short and Sweet 2

2 Barrel of Fun 3

3 Belongings. 4

4 Let's Stay Together 5

5 The Great and the Good 6

6 Famous Places 7

7 The Silver Screen 8

8 Food for Thought 9

9 Opposites Attract 10

10 Two's Company 11

11 Playing with Sayings 12

12 Food Hamper 13

13 You What? 14

14 What For?. 15

15 Different Quotes for Different Folks. 16

16 Sing Something Simple. 17

17 Name the Star 18

18 Tune in to Television 19

Contents

SHORT ANSWERS

1 All About Me. 22

2 Alphabet Game 23

3 Different Word, Same Meaning 24

4 On the Ball. 25

5 World Game 26

6 Size and Shape 27

7 Sniff it and See 28

8 Where might you find ...? 29

9 Job Descriptions. 30

10 Male and Female 31

11 Photographic Memory 32

12 Retail Therapy 33

13 Fictional Characters 34

14 Changing Rooms 35

15 What Comes to Mind?. 36

16 What, Where and Who? 37

17 Where Do You Put It?. 38

18 Who Said It? 39

LONGER ANSWERS

1 Name that Place 42

2 The Fame Game 43

3 The tools for the Job 44

4 Face the Facts 45

5 How do you do? 46

6 'I Went To …' 47

7 Guess the Pastime 48

8 Simon Says 49

9 What do you do with it? 50

10 Room Makeover 51

11 Highs and Lows 52

12 Role Playing 53

13 Cook up a Story 54

14 The Great Debate 56

15 Wacky Ways with Objects 57

16 What Happened Next? 58

17 Gizmos 59

18 Where or What Is It? 60

Contents

NON-VERBAL ACTIVITIES

1 A Piece of the Action 62

2 Blindfolds. 63

3 Do This, Do That. 64

4 Hive of Activity. 65

5 Sign for it. 66

6 Cacophony 67

7 Draw Your Feelings 67

8 Identification 68

9 Feely Bag 69

10 Look and Remember 69

11 Make a Face 70

12 Miming Matters 71

13 What's My Line? 72

14 Pass it on 73

15 Picture Bingo 74

16 In the Dark 76

17 Taste, Touch and Smell 77

18 Pass the Paper 78

READING

1 Match the Action 80

2 The Advertising Game 81

3 Sports Bingo 82

4 Room Bingo 83

5 Board Game 84

6 Comprehension Passages 86

7 Desert Island Discs 86

8 Double Name Game 87

9 Hitting the Headlines 88

10 Read the Label 88

11 Odd One Out 89

12 Cheesy Rhymes 90

13 Highway Code 91

14 Names to Faces 91

15 Summing Up 92

16 What Am I? 93

17 Country Bingo 94

18 Chain Letters 96

Contents

WRITING

1 A Day in the Life. 98

2 Free Association 99

3 Top Twenty 100

4 Book codes 101

5 Scrambled Songs. 102

6 Jumblies. 103

7 Pasty Faces 104

8 You're the Chef. 104

9 Same and Different 105

10 Storyline. 106

11 The Noun Game 107

12 The Adjective Game 108

13 Millionaire. 109

14 Dream Holiday 109

15 Heaven on Earth 110

16 Letting off Steam. 110

17 Secret Santa 111

18 Postbag 112

INTRODUCTION

This handbook of games and activities has been compiled for use by professionals, volunteers and carers in education, health and social settings; indeed, anyone responsible for organising group activities. The material is intended as a supplement to existing resources and is presented here in an easily accessible form.

The first edition, entitled *Activities and Ideas*, was published in 1983, and came out at a time when there were hardly any therapy materials on the market, and therapists spent considerable time putting together their own resources when they could have been spending more time with clients. The book became a bestseller, providing over one hundred ideas for word games and group activities. Many required little or no preparation beforehand, and others required only a flipchart, pen and paper.

We felt that many of the examples in the original edition had become outdated. *Crossroads* is no longer topping the ratings; *ER* is. Spotted dick has stopped being a staple of the British diet; ciabatta and pesto are today's replacements. Ronald Reagan and Margaret Thatcher are no longer stalking the corridors of power; instead, we are governed by the likes of Tony Blair and Arnie Schwarzenegger. So as well as dozens of new activities, this edition includes a completely new set of examples.

The instructions and examples are not meant to be followed slavishly. Do adapt them as you see fit and depending on the ability of the group. For example, with some groups you can introduce an element of competition: two teams racing to finish first, or scoring points for the correct answers. Above all, aim for enjoyment along the way.

ABOUT THE AUTHORS

Jayne Comins

A speech & language therapist and analytical psychologist who specialises in psychosocial aspects of communication, and voice disorders. She works in London at the Queen Elizabeth and Wellington Hospitals and in private practice.

Felicity Llewellyn

Qualified as a speech & language therapist in 1976, and worked in a variety of settings in London from 1976 to 1983. She has been employed at a community health centre in Dorset since that date.

Judith Offiler

Qualified in 1979 as a speech & language therapist, and worked in London until 1989 before moving to the north-east of England. She is currently working as a specialist with children and adults who have learning disabilities.

CUED
RESPONSES

1 Short and Sweet

Complete the following well-known abbreviations:

1	RIP	Rest in (Peace)
2	MOD	Ministry of (Defence)
3	VIP	Very Important (Person)
4	IMF	International Monetary (Fund)
5	AA	Alcoholics (Anonymous)/Automobile (Association)
6	EU	European (Union)
7	WC	Water (Closet)
8	WHO	World Health (Organization)
9	FO	Foreign (Office)
10	BA	Bachelor of (Arts)
11	ATC	Air Traffic (Control)
12	VW	Volks(wagen)
13	CD	Compact (Disk)
14	GBH	Grievous Bodily (Harm)
15	BO	Body (Odour)
16	MSG	Monosodium (Glutamate)
17	UK	United (Kingdom)
18	NY	New (York)
19	ER	Emergency (Room)
20	AD	Anno (Domini)
21	MPH	Miles per (Hour)
22	IBS	Irritable Bowel (Syndrome)
23	OAP	Old-Age (Pensioner)
24	SOB	Son of a (Bitch)
25	NYPD	New York Police (Department)
26	COD	Cash on (Delivery)
27	UN	United (Nations)
28	DOB	Date of (Birth)
29	MEP	Member of the European (Parliament)
30	DIY	Do it (Yourself)

2 A Barrel of Fun

Suggest suitable words to complete the following:

1   A vase of …
2   A spoonful of …
3   A litre of …
4   A band of …
5   A houseful of …
6   A metre of …
7   A gang of …
8   A pocketful of …
9   A carrier bag of …
10 A crate of …
11 A pinch of …
12 A fistful of …
13 A lorryload of …
14 A heap of …
15 A crock of …
16 A class of …
17 A shelf of …
18 A pod of …
19 A file of …
20 A list of …
21 A kilo of …
22 A brace of …
23 A constellation of …
24 A pack of …
25 A drawer of …
26 A roll of …
27 A book of …
28 A basket of …
29 A shot of …
30 A school of …

3 Belongings

Find the equivalent word to complete the sentence:

1   Mouse is to computer as aerial is to *(television)*
2   Hat is to head as sock is to *(foot)*
3   Rod is to fishing as racquet is to *(tennis)*
4   Snow is to skiing as ice is to *(skating)*
5   Bird is to nest as bee is to *(hive)*
6   Glasses are to eyes as hearing aid is to *(ear)*
7   Drink is to cup as food is to *(plate)*
8   Pedal is to bicycle as engine is to *(car)*
9   Wool is to sheep as feathers are to *(birds)*
10 Polar bear is to Arctic as kangaroo is to *(Australia)*
11 Cushion is to chair as pillow is to *(bed)*
12 London is to Britain as Paris is to *(France)*
13 Clothes are to humans as fur is to *(animals)*
14 Trousers are to legs as scarf is to *(neck)*
15 Bat is to baseball as cue is to *(snooker/billiards/pool)*
16 Spawn is to frog as egg is to *(chicken/bird)*
17 Doctor is to people as vet is to *(animals)*
18 Book is to read as television is to *(watch)*
19 Apple is to fruit as carrot is to *(vegetable)*
20 Brick is to wall as wood is to *(fence)*
21 Cheese is to biscuit as jam is to *(bread)*
22 Plane is to pilot as train is to *(driver)*
23 Plant is to pot as flower is to *(vase)*
24 Water is to sea as sand is to *(beach)*
25 Hand is to arm as head is to *(neck)*
26 Conductor is to orchestra as teacher is to *(class)*
27 Soy sauce is to noodles as pesto is to *(pasta)*
28 Mascara is to eyes as lipstick is to *(mouth)*
29 Fish is to pond as bird is to *(cage)*
30 Aborigine is to Australia as Maori is to *(New Zealand)*

4 Let's Stay Together

Supply the missing words in these well-known couples:

1 John F Kennedy and Jackie *(Onassis)*
2 Michael Douglas and Catherine Zeta *(Jones)*
3 George W and Laura *(Bush)*
4 Wallace and *(Grommit)*
5 The Lady and the *(Tramp)*
6 Anthony and *(Cleopatra)*
7 John Lennon and Yoko *(Ono)*
8 Porgy and *(Bess)*
9 Posh and *(Becks)*
10 Richard Burton and Elizabeth *(Taylor)*
11 Gilbert and *(Sullivan)*
12 Simon and *(Garfunkel)*
13 Homer and Marge *(Simpson)*
14 Basil and Sybil *(Fawlty)*
15 Romulus and *(Remus)*
16 Marks and *(Spencer)*
17 Margaret and Dennis *(Thatcher)*
18 Edward VIII and Wallis *(Simpson)*
19 Charles and *(Camilla)*
20 Thelma and *(Louise)*
21 Rudolf Nureyev and Margot *(Fonteyn)*
22 Superman and Lois *(Lane)*
23 Cain and *(Abel)*
24 Napoleon and *(Josephine)*
25 Prince Rainier and Princess *(Grace)*
26 Frank Sinatra and Ava *(Gardner)*
27 Mickey and Minnie *(Mouse)*
28 Ronnie Barker and Ronnie *(Corbett)*
29 Queen Elizabeth and Prince *(Philip)*
30 The Owl and the *(Pussycat)*

5 The Great and the Good

Supply the surnames of these well-known personalities. If people get stuck, occupations can be given as clues.

1 Celine (Dion) – Singer
2 Sir Edmund (Hillary) – Mountaineer
3 Neil (Armstrong) – Astronaut
4 Ronald (Reagan) – President
5 Winston (Churchill) – Prime Minister
6 Marco (Polo) – Explorer
7 Marlene (Dietrich) – Actress
8 Arnold (Schwarzenegger) – Actor/Governor of California
9 Marlon (Brando) – Actor
10 Elton (John) – Singer
11 Whoopi (Goldberg) – Actress
12 Marilyn (Monroe) – Actress
13 Ringo (Starr) – Beatle
14 Oprah (Winfrey) – Chat Show Host
15 Raquel (Welch) – Actress
16 Nelson (Mandela) – (Former) President of South Africa
17 Martin Luther (King) – Civil Rights Campaigner
18 Kiri (Te Kanawa) – Opera Singer
19 Brigitte (Bardot) – Actress
20 Vincent (van Gogh) – Artist
21 Salvador (Dali) – Artist
22 Luciano (Pavarotti) – Opera Singer
23 Johnny (Wilkinson) – Rugby Player
24 Sir Roger (Bannister) – Athlete
25 Jerry (Springer) – Chat Show Host
26 Orson (Welles) – Actor/Director
27 Emmeline (Pankhurst) – Suffragette
28 Oswald (Moseley) – Fascist Leader
29 Germaine (Greer) – Writer/Broadcaster
30 Robbie (Williams) – Singer

6 Famous Places

Supply the last part of the names of these places:

1   Yellowstone National (Park)
2   The Wailing (Wall)
3   The Tower of (London)
4   Silicone (Valley)
5   Tiananmen (Square)
6   Sydney Opera (House)
7   The Dome of the (Rock)
8   The Giant's (Causeway)
9   The Lake (District)
10 The Sistine (Chapel)
11 The Persian (Gulf)
12 Sunset (Boulevard)
13 The Sahara (Desert)
14 The Great Wall of (China)
15 The Leaning Tower of (Pisa)
16 The Empire State (Building)
17 The Golden Gate (Bridge)
18 Fifth (Avenue)
19 Bondi (Beach)
20 The Atlantic (Ocean)
21 Disney (World)
22 Hadrian's (Wall)
23 Piccadilly (Circus)
24 The Forbidden (City)
25 The Millennium (Dome/Bridge)
26 The Eden (Project)
27 The Costa (Brava/Blanca/Del Sol)
28 Salt Lake (City)
29 The Kennedy Space (Center)
30 Grand Central (Station)

7 The Silver Screen

Complete the titles of these well-known films:

1 *Citizen (Kane)*
2 *A Clockwork (Orange)*
3 *Planet of the (Apes)*
4 2001 *A Space (Odyssey)*
5 198(4)
6 *Silence of the (Lambs)*
7 *Twelve Angry (Men)*
8 *Chitty Chitty (Bang Bang)*
9 *The Wizard of (Oz)*
10 *Four Weddings and a (Funeral)*
11 *The Full (Monty)*
12 *Annie Get Your (Gun)*
13 *All the President's (Men)*
14 *One Hundred and One (Dalmatians)*
15 *Schindler's (List)*
16 *Chicken (Run)*
17 *The Lion (King)*
18 *It's a Wonderful (Life)*
19 *Singing in the (Rain)*
20 *Diamonds are (Forever)*
21 *An Officer and a (Gentleman)*
22 *Mission (Impossible)*
23 *The Elephant (Man)*
24 *The Empire Strikes (Back)*
25 *Assault on Precinct* (13)
26 *Blade (Runner)*
27 *Apocalypse (Now)*
28 *Raiders of the Lost (Ark)*
29 *Monty Python's Life of (Brian)*
30 *Invasion of the Body (Snatchers)*

8 Food for Thought

Complete the names of these items of food.
(Answers are only suggestions – there may be alternatives.)

1   Maple (syrup)
2   Shepherd's (pie)
3   Orange (juice)
4   Hot (dog)
5   Prawn (cocktail)
6   Spaghetti (bolognese)
7   French (fries)
8   Baked (beans)
9   Peach (melba)
10 Cauliflower (cheese)
11 Pâté de foie (gras)
12 Waldorf (salad)
13 Espresso (coffee)
14 Banana (custard)
15 Roast (potatoes)
16 Horseradish (sauce)
17 Olive (oil)
18 Pork (chop)
19 Sun-dried (tomatoes)
20 Macaroni (cheese)
21 Cole (slaw)
22 Peking (duck)
23 Dim (sum)
24 Deep pan (pizza)
25 Onion (bhajee)
26 Jumbo (prawns)
27 Mozzarella (cheese)
28 Scrambled (egg)
29 Sponge (cake)
30 Fromage (frais)

9 Opposites Attract

Give the opposite of each of the following words:

1 Dry and (wet)
2 Full and (empty)
3 Man and (woman)
4 Inside and (outside)
5 East and (west)
6 Top and (bottom)
7 Early and (late)
8 Dawn and (dusk)
9 Strong and (weak)
10 Push and (pull)
11 Girl and (boy)
12 Stop and (go)
13 Over and (under)
14 Fast and (slow)
15 Thin and (thick)
16 Large and (small)
17 Hard and (soft)
18 New and (old)
19 Cheap and (expensive)
20 Spring and (autumn)
21 Huge and (tiny)
22 Beginning and (end)
23 Near and (far)
24 Curly and (straight)
25 Convex and (concave)
26 Love and (hate)
27 Husband and (wife)
28 Birth and (death)
29 Difficult and (easy)
30 Pessimistic and (optimistic)

10 Two's Company

Give the word most likely to complete the pair. *(There may be more than one possible answer.)*

1 Bucket and *(spade)*
2 Martini and *(lemonade)*
3 Rum and *(coke)*
4 Hell and high *(water)*
5 Pie and *(mash)*
6 Chalk and *(cheese)*
7 Hammer and *(nails)*
8 Rock and *(roll)*
9 Nuts and *(raisins)*
10 Salt and *(pepper/vinegar)*
11 Needle and *(thread)*
12 Fruit and *(nut)*
13 Stars and *(stripes)*
14 Peaches and *(cream)*
15 Fish and *(chips)*
16 Vodka and *(tonic/lime/orange)*
17 Needle and *(thread)*
18 Anvil and *(hammer)*
19 Pestle and *(mortar)*
20 Shirt and *(tie)*
21 Doctors and *(nurses)*
22 Bra and *(pants/knickers/underwear)*
23 Television and *(radio)*
24 Stamp and *(envelope)*
25 Arms and *(legs)*
26 Rose and *(crown)*
27 Apples and *(pears/oranges)*
28 Top hat and *(tails)*
29 Bride and *(groom)*
30 Doom and *(gloom)*

11 Playing with Sayings

Supply the final words of these well-known phrases.

1   It never rains but it (pours)
2   It's all or (nothing)
3   Don't rock the (boat)
4   Close the stable door after the horse has (bolted)
5   A pain in the (neck)
6   I'll eat my (hat)
7   Look after the pennies and the pounds will look after (themselves)
8   Don't run before you can (walk)
9   People in glass houses shouldn't throw (stones)
10 Don't cry over spilt (milk)
11 Anything for a quiet (life)
12 As sick as a (parrot)
13 To build castles in the (air)
14 Empty vessels make the most (noise)
15 Beauty is but skin (deep)
16 To flog a dead (horse)
17 Like a fish out of (water)
18 Better be safe than (sorry)
19 To hit the nail on the (head)
20 He wouldn't say boo to a (goose)
21 Great minds think (alike)
22 A cat has nine (lives)
23 Cut your coat according to your (cloth)
24 Like a house on (fire)
25 Let bygones be (bygones)
26 Ask no questions, tell no (lies)
27 Like father, like (son)
28 Business before (pleasure)
29 Age before (beauty)
30 An apple a day keeps the doctor (away)

12 Food Hamper

Fill in the missing words in these well-known food and drink brands.

1 Kentucky Fried (Chicken)
2 McVitie's Chocolate (Digestives)
3 HP (Sauce)
4 Sarson's Malt (Vinegar)
5 Hellman's (Mayonnaise)
6 Heinz Baked (Beans)
7 Twinings (Tea)
8 Nescafé Gold (Blend)
9 Terry's Chocolate (Orange)
10 Pepsi (Cola)
11 Cadbury's Milk (Tray)
12 Ben and Jerry's Ice (Cream)
13 Bird's Eye Fish (Fingers)
14 McDonald's Big (Mac)
15 Jacob's Cream (Crackers)
16 Wrigley's Spearmint (Gum)
17 Ambrosia Creamed Rice (Pudding)
18 Stone's Green (Ginger Wine)
19 Branston (Pickle)
20 Batchelor's Cup-A-(Soup)
21 Tiptree Orange (Marmalade)
22 Bailey's Irish (Cream)
23 Robinson's Barley (Water)
24 Fray Bentos Steak and Kidney (Pie)
25 Carling Black (Label)
26 Quaker Porridge (Oats)
27 Lurpak Danish (Butter)
28 Tate & Lyle Golden (Syrup)
29 Kellogg's Rice (Krispies)
30 Harvey's Bristol (Cream)

13 You What?

Suggest suitable words to complete these sentences:

1   You mow …

2   You grate …

3   You suck …

4   You throw …

5   You rob …

6   You blow …

7   You fry …

8   You run …

9   You teach …

10   You save …

11   You sign …

12   You look …

13   You peel …

14   You sleep …

15   You give …

16   You think …

17   You jump …

18   You spend …

19   You row …

20   You sit …

21   You iron …

22   You fire …

23   You chase …

24   You drive …

25   You dig …

26   You dance …

27   You kick …

28   You butter …

29   You compose …

30   You score …

14 What For?

Find suitable words to complete these sentences:

1   Perfume is for …
2   A clock is for …
3   A television is for …
4   A radio is for …
5   A newspaper is for …
6   Scissors are for …
7   A suitcase is for …
8   Lipstick is for …
9   A bell is for …
10   A vacuum cleaner is for …
11   A microwave is for …
12   A CD is for …
13   Shoes are for …
14   Hooks are for …
15   Teeth are for …
16   A cup is for …
17   Trees are for …
18   Milk is for …
19   A marathon is for …
20   A spade is for …
21   A fridge is for …
22   Boxes are for …
23   Butter is for …
24   Guns are for …
25   A door is for …
26   A ball is for …
27   A song is for …
28   Clothes are for …
29   Postcards are for …
30   A candle is for …

15 Different Quotes for Different Folks

Complete these quotations:

1 I came, I saw, I *(conquered)*
2 Nearer my God to *(thee)*
3 Guinness is good for *(you)*
4 My bonny lies over the *(ocean)*
5 There's a sucker born every *(minute)*
6 A land flowing with milk and *(honey)*
7 Stands the church clock at ten to three, and is there honey still for *(tea)*?
8 The Queen of Hearts, she made some *(tarts)*
9 Elementary, my dear *(Watson)*
10 This was their finest *(hour)*
11 I think, therefore I *(am)*
12 Goodbye to all *(that)*
13 Peace in our *(time)*
14 To be, or not to *(be)*
15 Mad, bad, and dangerous to *(know)*
16 In the bleak *(midwinter)*
17 The boy stood on the burning *(deck)*
18 A life on the ocean *(wave)*
19 East is east and west is *(west)*
20 Other men live to eat, whereas I eat to *(live)*
21 Go west, young *(man)*
22 Dr Livingstone, I *(presume)*?
23 John Brown's body lies a-mouldering in the *(grave)*
24 If music be the food of *(love)*
25 Come up and see me *(sometime)*
26 Isn't it funny how a bear likes *(honey)*?
27 Gentlemen prefer *(blondes)*
28 Survival of the *(fittest)*
29 You've never had it so *(good)*
30 Your country needs *(you)*

16 Sing Something Simple

Fill in the missing word and/or sing a few bars of each song:

1 Oh, when the saints go marching *(in)*
2 My old man's a *(dustman)*
3 She loves you *(yeah, yeah, yeah)*
4 There'll be blue birds over the white cliffs of *(Dover)*
5 Land of hope and *(glory)*
6 I'm dreaming of a white *(Christmas)*
7 The hills are alive with the sound of *(music)*
8 I could have danced all *(night)*
9 Bridge over troubled *(water)*
10 Blue suede *(shoes)*
11 Goodbye yellow brick *(road)*
12 We all live in a yellow *(submarine)*
13 Nessun *(dorma)*
14 Maria, I once kissed a girl called *(Maria)*
15 Somewhere over the *(rainbow)*
16 I am sixteen, going on *(seventeen)*
17 As time goes *(by)*
18 Tiptoe through the *(tulips)*
19 Bess you is my *(woman)*
20 I can't get no *(satisfaction)*
21 London Bridge is falling *(down)*
22 Do you know the way to San *(Jose)*?
23 Away in a *(manger)*
24 All things bright and *(beautiful)*
25 Every time we say *(goodbye)*
26 Let's face the music and *(dance)*
27 It's been a hard day's *(night)*
28 Raindrops keep falling on my *(head)*
29 How long has this been going *(on)*?
30 You'll never walk *(alone)*

17 Name the Star

Complete the following names of famous actors and actresses:

1   Harrison (Ford)
2   Brad (Pitt)
3   Sylvester (Stallone)
4   Al (Pacino)
5   Helena Bonham (Carter)
6   Nicole (Kidman)
7   Sean (Connery)
8   Meryl (Streep)
9   Elizabeth (Taylor)
10 Marlene (Dietrich)
11 Humphrey (Bogart)
12 Lauren (Bacall)
13 Woody (Allen)
14 Catherine Zeta (Jones)
15 Hugh (Grant)
16 Jude (Law)
17 Cameron (Diaz)
18 Demi (Moore)
19 Russell (Crowe)
20 Ewan (McGregor)
21 Halle (Berry)
22 Johnny (Depp)
23 Jodie (Foster)
24 Clint (Eastwood)
25 Charlie (Chaplin, Sheen)
26 Eddie (Murphy)
27 Audrey (Hepburn)
28 Judy (Garland)
29 Sidney (Poitier)
30 Grace (Kelly)

18 Tune in to Television

Give the last word of the titles of these popular television programmes:

1 Star (Trek)
2 Inspector (Morse)
3 Changing (Rooms)
4 Ground (Force)
5 The West (Wing)
6 Buffy the Vampire (Slayer)
7 The X (Files)
8 Coronation (Street)
9 The Oprah (Winfrey Show)
10 Who Wants To Be A (Millionaire)?
11 Absolutely (Fabulous)
12 Fawlty (Towers)
13 Antiques (Roadshow)
14 The Jerry Springer (Show)
15 Home and (Away)
16 East (Enders)
17 E (R)
18 How Clean is Your (House)?
19 The Weakest (Link)
20 A Touch of (Frost)
21 Breakfast with (Frost)
22 Ready Steady (Cook/Go)
23 Only Fools and (Horses)
24 Bill and (Ben)
25 Men Behaving (Badly)
26 Holby (City)
27 Antiques (Roadshow)
28 Bob the (Builder)
29 Match of the (Day)
30 What Not to (Wear)

SHORT
ANSWERS

1 All About Me

Add a word or phrase to complete these statements:

1   My name is …
2   I was born in …
3   I live in …
4   My age is …
5   I get up in the morning at …
6   I like to go to bed at …
7   My favourite food is …
8   I like to drink …
9   My favourite television programme is …
10 I like weather that is …
11 My favourite month is …
12 I'd like to go on holiday to …
13 I like the colour …
14 My favourite pet animal is …
15 My favourite music is …
16 I don't like weather that is …
17 I don't like to feel …
18 I don't like the smell of …
19 I don't like to eat …
20 I don't like people who …
21 Today I am …
22 Yesterday I …
23 Tomorrow I will …
24 Last week I …
25 Next week I …
26 My last job was …
27 In my spare time I like to …
28 My favourite shop is …
29 On Sundays I like to …
30 If I won the lottery I would …

2 Alphabet Game

Give an example of each of these items, beginning with 'A', then 'B', then 'C', and working through the alphabet around the group. It doesn't matter if you can't think of 26.

1   Sports team (Arsenal, Barnsley, Charlton, etc.)
2   Plant or tree
3   First name
4   Body part
5   Herb or spice
6   Animal
7   Sport or game
8   Holiday destination
9   Hobby
10 Surname/family name

3 Different Word, Same Meaning

Think of a word that is similar in meaning to each of the following. (The answers given are only suggestions.)

1 Lovely (beautiful)
2 Trap (catch)
3 Crafty (wily)
4 Icy (frozen)
5 Packed (crammed)
6 Observe (watch)
7 Tear (rip)
8 Slither (slide)
9 Drop (fall)
10 Sprint (run)
11 Bouquet (bunch)
12 Branch (bough)
13 Adult (grown-up)
14 Cloth (fabric)
15 Destroy (wreck)
16 Family (relatives)
17 Famous (well-known)
18 Perfect (ideal)
19 Stone (pebble)
20 Start (begin)
21 Child (kid)
22 Expensive (dear)
23 Tetchy (grumpy)
24 Tough (hard)
25 Sensitive (touchy)
26 Crazy (mad)
27 Glad (pleased)
28 Deceitful (dishonest)
29 Devout (religious)
30 Affluent (rich)

4 On the Ball

Have group members throw a ball or beanbag to one another, as quickly as possible for their level of ability. The person who catches it must answer one of the following questions.

1   If you were a car, what would you be?
2   What is your shoe size?
3   If you were a famous person, who would you be?
4   Where do you live?
5   If you were an animal, what would you be?
6   What is your favourite food?
7   How are you feeling today?
8   What is your favourite drink?
9   What is the name of the prime minister/president?
10 What is your favourite colour?
11 What is the weather like today?
12 What do you think the weather will be like tomorrow?
13 Do you have any brothers or sisters?
14 What was the last television programme you watched?
15 What do you think of capital punishment?
16 Who is the funniest comedian ever?
17 Where is the nearest railway station?
18 Do you come here often?
19 What is the capital of Scotland?
20 How many days in a year?

5 World Game

What are these tourist attractions famous for?
(Answers given are only suggestions.)

1 The London Eye (views over London)
2 The left bank of the Seine (artists)
3 Fortnum and Mason (food)
4 Rio de Janeiro (carnival)
5 The Tower of London (crown jewels/beefeaters/ravens)
6 Mount Everest (tallest mountain)
7 Notting Hill (carnival)
8 The Vatican (pope)
9 Loch Ness (monster)
10 Waikiki beach (surfing)
11 Stratford-upon-Avon (Shakespeare)
12 Gretna Green (marriages)
13 Lourdes (pilgrimages)
14 Madame Tussauds (waxworks)
15 Brands Hatch (motor racing)
16 Windsor (castle)
17 Number 10, Downing Street (prime minister's residence)
18 Oxford (university)
19 Washington DC (White House)
20 Las Vegas (gambling)
21 The Oval (cricket ground)
22 Great Barrier Reef (coral/diving)
23 Nashville (country and western music)
24 Alcatraz (prison)
25 Memphis (Elvis)
26 Orlando (Disney World)
27 Klosters (skiing)
28 Amsterdam (tulips/red light district)
29 Venice (canals)
30 Black Forest (gateau)

6 Size and Shape

Suggest things that are associated with each size or shape,
eg, round – hole; square – box; long – pole.

1 Round
2 Long
3 Square
4 Triangular
5 Short
6 Wide
7 Thin
8 Fat
9 Pointy
10 Oval
11 Narrow
12 Broad
13 Rectangular
14 Sharp
15 Flat
16 Tiny
17 Bumpy
18 Baggy
19 Symmetrical
20 Rough
21 Huge
22 Spiky
23 Crooked
24 Blunt
25 Jagged
26 Hollow
27 Tall
28 Knobbly
29 Tapering
30 Curved

7 Sniff it and See

Place items with distinctive smells in boxes and then pass them around the group. Members take turns to identify each item while their eyes are closed. If they can't guess it, the item is passed on to the next person.

Some suggestions:
  Pepper
  Lavender
  Mothballs
  Scented soap
  Antiseptic
  Rose oil
  Herbs
  Garlic
  Cheese
  Fish

8 Where might you find …?

Where might you find a …? (Answers given are only suggestions).

1 Family (house)
2 Tourist (hotel)
3 Hamster (cage)
4 Cow (field)
5 Sloth (tree)
6 Whale (sea)
7 Camper (tent)
8 Termite (anthill/mound)
9 Tadpole (pond)
10 Lion (den)
11 Farmer (farmhouse)
12 Native American (tepee)
13 Aeroplane (hangar)
14 Lion tamer (circus)
15 Police officer (police station)
16 Nurse (hospital)
17 Teacher (school)
18 King (palace)
19 Plant (pot)
20 Cooker (kitchen)
21 Car (garage)
22 Doll (doll's house)
23 Match (box)
24 Nib (pen)
25 Piece of software (computer)
26 Driver (car)
27 Bath (bathroom)
28 Haystack (field)
29 Bullet (gun)
30 Cork (bottle)

9 Job Descriptions

What do we call the people who have these occupations?
(Other answers are possible).

1 I ride horses in races (jockey)
2 I do a job for no money (volunteer)
3 I paint your house (decorator)
4 I check your pulse (doctor)
5 I book you into the hotel (receptionist)
6 I arrange your holiday (travel agent)
7 I appear on stage and in films (actor)
8 I play music on a radio station (disc jockey)
9 I sell flowers (florist)
10 I look at your feet (chiropodist, podiatrist)
11 I cut your hair (hairdresser, barber)
12 I put you in a trance (hypnotist)
13 I carry your bags (porter)
14 I mend your fuse (electrician)
15 I look after your children while you are at work (childminder, nanny)
16 I drive you and take payment (taxi driver)
17 I perform tricks (conjuror)
18 I prepare your meals in a restaurant (chef, cook)
19 I wash floors for money (cleaner)
20 I help sick animals (vet)
21 I look after parks and gardens (gardener)
22 I make sure sports players keep to the rules (referee, umpire)
23 I catch fish (fisherman, angler)
24 I make clothes (tailor)
25 I mend your broken car (mechanic)
26 I help you sell your house (estate agent)
27 I tell your future by looking at the stars (astrologer)
28 I do experiments (scientist)
29 I design buildings (architect)
30 I fly into space (astronaut)

10 Male and Female

Name the opposite-sex version of each of the following.

1 Count *(countess)*

2 Policeman *(policewoman)*

3 Host *(hostess)*

4 Madame *(monsieur)*

5 Ladies *(gentlemen)*

6 Duck *(drake)*

7 God *(goddess)*

8 Brother *(sister)*

9 Baron *(baroness)*

10 Witch *(wizard, warlock)*

11 Masseur *(masseuse)*

12 Manservant *(maidservant)*

13 Emperor *(empress)*

14 Master *(mistress)*

15 Mr *(Mrs)*

16 Sportsman *(sportswoman)*

17 Waiter *(waitress)*

18 Son *(daughter)*

19 Chairman *(chairwoman)*

20 Grandmother *(grandfather)*

11 Photographic Memory

Pass a selection of photographs around the group or give everyone a copy of the same picture.

Ask the group to study the picture(s), and then after a set time turn them face down.

Ask each group member in turn to describe their picture or tell the group one thing they remember from the picture.

12 Retail Therapy

What products are the following manufacturers well known for?
(The answers given are only suggestions.)

1 IKEA (furniture)
2 B&Q (DIY products)
3 Dixons (electrical goods)
4 Clark's (shoes)
5 Johnson's (baby products)
6 Jaeger (clothes)
7 Adidas (sports gear)
8 Levi's (jeans)
9 Rolex (watches)
10 Campbell's (soup)
11 Body Shop (toiletries)
12 Nike (sports wear)
13 Hertz (car hire)
14 Hilton (hotels)
15 Fosters (lager)
16 Marks and Spencer (clothes, food and household items)
17 Fortnum and Mason (food)
18 Marlboro (cigarettes)
19 Schweppes (soft drinks)
20 BMW (cars)
21 Boeing (planes)
22 Wella (shampoo)
23 Cartier (jewellery)
24 Samsonite (luggage)
25 Nikon (cameras)
26 Kodak (film)
27 Estée Lauder (cosmetics)
28 Harley Davidson (motorbikes)
29 Burberry (clothing)
30 WH Smith (books, stationery)

13 Fictional Characters

In which book, play, film or television programme do these characters appear?

1 Darth Vader (the *Star Wars* movies)
2 Olive Oyl (*Popeye*)
3 Iago (*Othello*)
4 Hannibal Lecter (*Silence of the Lambs|Hannibal|Red Dragon*)
5 Laa-Laa ('Teletubbies')
6 Homer (*The Simpsons*)
7 Lady Penelope ('Thunderbirds')
8 Tigger (*Winnie the Pooh*)
9 Inspector Clouseau (*Pink Panther*)
10 Elizabeth Bennett (*Pride and Prejudice*)
11 Miss Moneypenny (James Bond stories)
12 Freddy Kruger (*Nightmare on Elm Street*)
13 Ron Weasley (Harry Potter novels)
14 Kermit the Frog (*The Muppets*)
15 Dana Scully ('The X Files')
16 Cordelia (*King Lear*)
17 Sam Spade (*Casablanca*)
18 Dozy (*Snow White and the Seven Dwarfs*)
19 J.R. Ewing ('Dallas')
20 Mrs Robinson (*The Graduate*)
21 Mr Toad ('The Wind in the Willows')
22 Tom and Barbara Good ('The Good Life')
23 Miss Havisham (*Great Expectations*)
24 Emma Peel ('The Avengers')
25 Edina ('Absolutely Fabulous')
26 David Brent ('The Office')
27 Frodo Baggins (*The Lord of the Rings*)
28 Rigsby ('Rising Damp')
29 Charlie Fairhead ('Casualty')
30 Maid Marian (*Robin Hood*)

14 Changing Rooms

Lead the group into a room and give them a set time to study it and try to remember as much as they can about it.

Ask the group to leave the room and then change five things (more or fewer can be changed, depending on the group's abilities.)

Once the changes have been made, invite the group back into the room and ask them to guess what changes have been made.

15 What Comes to Mind?

Ask group members to think of as many words as possible to describe the following items. Some will be more difficult than others.

1 Cinnamon
2 Fudge
3 Record player
4 Telegram
5 Barbed wire
6 Sandpit
7 Hot dog
8 Torch
9 Candle
10 Cotton wool
11 Vinyl record
12 Tram
13 Typewriter
14 Diamond ring
15 Cushion
16 Suntan lotion
17 Money belt
18 Ice
19 Garden
20 Passport
21 Chocolate
22 Snake
23 Thunder
24 Sea
25 Mountain
26 Aeroplane
27 Milk
28 Mouse
29 Bank
30 Orange

16 What, Where and Who?

Give short answers to the following questions.
(The answers given are only suggestions.)

1 What do you need to light a fire? *(matches)*
2 Where do you catch a train from? *(station)*
3 Who delivers mail? *(postman/woman)*
4 What do you sleep on? *(bed)*
5 Where might you use chopsticks? *(Chinese restaurant)*
6 Who makes speeches? *(politician)*
7 What do you do with a doughnut? *(eat it)*
8 Where do you put dentures? *(in your mouth)*
9 Who looks after sick animals? *(vet)*
10 What is a jug for? *(holding water)*
11 What do you wear on your hands? *(gloves)*
12 Where do you see films? *(cinema)*
13 Who wears a crown? *(king, queen, royalty)*
14 What do you use for cutting the lawn? *(lawnmower)*
15 Where do you cook breakfast? *(kitchen)*
16 Who flies a plane? *(pilot)*
17 What do you keep in a purse? *(money)*
18 Where do you keep milk? *(fridge)*
19 Who looks after your teeth? *(dentist)*
20 What makes you laugh? *(jokes)*
21 Where would you go for a meal? *(restaurant)*
22 Who writes the news in a paper? *(journalist)*
23 What illness do you often get in winter? *(cold)*
24 When is New Year? *(1st January)*
25 Who takes photographs at a wedding? *(photographer)*
26 What do you often do when you're asleep? *(dream)*
27 When was the Battle of Hastings? *(1066)*
28 Who paints pictures? *(artist)*
29 What do you call someone who doesn't tell the truth? *(liar)*
30 Where is Edinburgh? *(Scotland)*

17 Where Do You Put It?

Where are these items found, or where do they belong?

1 Milk
2 Rake
3 Petrol
4 Wine
5 Duvet
6 Caravan
7 Suitcase
8 Bicycle
9 Television
10 CD
11 Cheese
12 Clothes
13 Plate
14 Letter
15 Goldfish
16 Curtains
17 Spade
18 Biscuit
19 In-tray
20 Fruit
21 Matches
22 Yacht
23 Horse
24 Photograph
25 Candle
26 Slippers
27 Cushion
28 Spectacles
29 Rubbish
30 Medicine

18 Who Said It?

1 'Read my lips' (George Bush)
2 'The lady's not for turning' (Margaret Thatcher)
3 'There will be no whitewash in the White House' (Richard Nixon)
4 'One small step for man, one giant leap for mankind' (Neil Armstrong)
5 'Kiss me, Hardy' (Horatio Nelson)
6 'You are the weakest link' (Anne Robinson)
7 'I have a dream' (Martin Luther King)
8 'Most of our people have never had it so good' (Harold Macmillan)
9 'I don't want to belong to any club that will accept me as a member' (Groucho Marx)
10 'Holy smoke!' (Batman)
11 'Ask not what your country can do for you; ask what you can do for your country' (John F Kennedy)
12 'I'll be back' (Arnold Schwarzenegger in *The Terminator*)
13 'Martini, shaken not stirred' (James Bond)
14 'I tort I saw a puddycat' (Tweety Pie)
15 'Is that a gun in your pocket, or are you just happy to see me?' (Mae West)
16 'This was their finest hour' (Winston Churchill)
17 '1992 … has turned out to be an *annus horribilis*' (Queen Elizabeth II)
18 'I came, I saw, I conquered' (Julius Caesar)
19 'Big Brother is watching you' (George Orwell)
20 'Curiouser and curiouser!' (Alice in Wonderland)
21 'Double, double, toil and trouble' (The witches in *Macbeth*)
22 'I take my man Friday with me' (Robinson Crusoe)
23 'Who loves ya baby?' (Kojak)
24 'Religion is the opium of the people' (Karl Marx)
25 'The owl and the pussycat went to sea in a beautiful pea-green boat' (Edward Lear)
26 'Eureka!' (Archimedes)

Short Answers

27 'We are not amused' (Queen Victoria)
28 'I did not have sexual relations with that woman' (Bill Clinton)
29 'Don't mention the war' (Basil Fawlty)
30 'Doh!' (Homer Simpson)

LONGER ANSWERS

1 Name that Place

The following are suggestions for games based on pictures of famous places cut out and pasted onto card.

1 What name?
   What is the name of the building? …city? …monument? …park?

2 What country?
   Name the country where it is.

3 What else?
   What else can you say about the picture?

4 Where is it near?
   Try to find out names of other buildings, famous places round about or belonging to that country.

2 The Fame Game

What are the following people famous for? Try to expand answers by asking for more information, such as what film the person appeared in.

1 Whoopee Goldberg (acting)
2 Ranulph Fiennes (exploring)
3 A. A. Milne (writing *Winnie the Pooh*)
4 Nelson Mandela (politics in South Africa)
5 Elizabeth Taylor (acting)
6 Stephen Hawking (physics)
7 Michael Schumacher (Formula One driving)
8 Luciano Pavarotti (opera singing)
9 Sir Andrew Lloyd Webber (composing)
10 William Shakespeare (writing plays)
11 Arnold Schwarzenegger (acting, politics)
12 Twiggy (modelling, singing, acting)
13 Indira Gandhi (Indian politician)
14 Shirley Bassey (singing)
15 David Hockney (art)
16 Jade Jagger (modelling, daughter of Mick Jagger)
17 Stella McCartney (designing clothes, daughter of Paul McCartney)
18 Billy Graham (evangelist)
19 Jeffrey Archer (author)
20 George W. Bush (US president)
21 Margaret Thatcher (former prime minister)
22 Walt Disney (cartoons)
23 Madonna (singing)
24 Bill Gates (computing)
25 Mike Tyson (boxing)
26 David Beckham (football)
27 Barbara Cartland (romantic novelist)
28 Joan Rivers (comedienne)
29 Mother Theresa (charity work)
30 Ronald Biggs (Great Train Robbery)

3 The tools for the Job

What equipment or tools would be needed to do the following?

1 Cut the grass
2 Wash the car
3 Put up a tent
4 Watch a video
5 Fax a message
6 Clean the bath
7 Make a sandwich
8 Take a photo
9 Wash your hair
10 Change a tyre
11 Mend a broken vase
12 Hang a picture
13 Sharpen a pencil
14 Mend a fuse
15 Set up a barbecue
16 Clean the windows
17 Paint a room
18 Send out party invitations
19 Mend a broken pane of glass
20 Make a bonfire
21 Prepare a picnic
22 Remove a coffee stain from a white shirt
23 Cut someone's hair
24 Grow tomatoes
25 Make a pizza
26 Play golf
27 Access the internet
28 Catch a fish
29 Decorate a Christmas tree
30 Write a book

4 **Face the Facts**

The following are suggestions for games based on photographs of faces cut out from magazines or newspapers or brought in by members.

1 *Famous faces*
   Group members are asked to identify the people concerned and describe what they do.

2 *Which member?*
   The group bring in early photographs of themselves for the others to identify.

3 *Relatives*
   People bring in photographs of their family members for the others to identify and discuss.

4 *What are they like?*
   The group are shown unfamiliar faces and have to describe what they are like, what they might do, etc.

5 How do you do?

Describe how to perform the following tasks:

1   Make a video
2   Rob a bank
3   Wash a car
4   Cut the grass
5   Open a bottle of wine
6   Clean your teeth
7   Make a pancake
8   Sew on a button
9   Make a doctor's appointment
10 Make a cashpoint withdrawal
11 Fill a fountain pen
12 Do the washing up
13 Make a photocopy
14 Forge a signature
15 Make chips
16 Go through airport security
17 Make a cocktail
18 Paint a wall
19 Put on makeup
20 Dye your hair
21 Clean your shoes
22 Grow daffodils
23 Make coffee
24 Send an email
25 Make a bonfire
26 Feed a dog
27 Make bread
28 Clean an oven
29 Buy a lottery ticket
30 Play a CD

6 'I Went To …'

The group leader starts off, 'I went to the … and bought/took some …'
Each person has to repeat the sentence and add an item when it is
their turn:

1 'I went to the supermarket and bought …'
2 'I went to the travel agent and booked …'
3 'I went on a picnic and ate …'
4 'I went on a cruise and saw …'
5 'I went up a mountain and saw …'
6 'I went to the seaside and bought …'
7 'I went to the sports centre and played …'
8 'I went on a holiday and had …'
9 'I went for a walk and saw …'
10 'I went to hospital and had …'
11 'I went to the cinema and saw …'
12 'I went to the gym and did …'
13 'I went to karaoke and sang …'
14 'I went to the beach and played …'
15 'I went to the sale and bought …'
16 'I went to the airport and saw …'
17 'I went to the chemist and asked for …'
18 'I went to the garden centre and bought …'
19 'I went to the circus and saw …'
20 'I went to the dentist and had …'
21 'I went to an art gallery and saw …'
22 'I went to the theatre and saw …'
23 'I went to Wimbledon and saw …'
24 'I went to the pier and played …'
25 'I went to the moon and saw …'
26 'I went to the bottom of the sea and saw …'
27 'I went to the nursery and saw …'
28 'I went on a safari and saw …'
29 'I went to a farm and bought …'
30 'I went to a party and met …'

7 Guess the Pastime

Each person has a hobby or sport written on a card, or in picture form. They have to describe the activity involved without mentioning its name:

1   Bungee jumping
2   Cycling
3   DIY
4   Playing the piano
5   Surfing
6   Cake decorating
7   Rowing
8   Yoga
9   Singing
10 Dressmaking
11 Jigsaws
12 Roller hockey
13 Belly dancing
14 Aerobics
15 Computer games
16 Judo
17 Tai chi
18 Skating
19 Mountaineering
20 Skiing
21 Drawing
22 Archery
23 Morris dancing
24 Snooker
25 Weaving
26 Ballroom dancing
27 Karaoke
28 Bridge
29 Paintballing
30 Crosswords

8 Simon Says

Each person in turn asks another member of the group to do something starting with 'Simon says …'

For example: 'Simon says touch your ears'.
'Simon says point to the door'.
'Simon says clap your hands'.

9 What do you do with it?

What are the following objects used for?

1   Corkscrew
2   Diary
3   Whisk
4   Compass
5   Calculator
6   Dictionary
7   Padlock
8   Address book
9   Ladder
10   Vase
11   String
12   Spoon
13   Credit card
14   Telescope
15   Freezer
16   Chequebook
17   Barbecue
18   Spade
19   Paperclip
20   Kettle
21   Iron
22   Remote control
23   Computer
24   Thermometer
25   Candle
26   Stapler
27   Telephone
28   Key
29   Smoke detector
30   Hamper

10 Room Makeover

Look at each main item in the room, for example chairs, curtains and tables. Discuss possible improvements to each, and what you would like to have if money were no object.

11 Highs and Lows

Describe what you would do if:

1 The doorbell rang in the middle of the night
2 The television broke down
3 Your vacuum cleaner needed emptying
4 Your house flooded
5 You won the lottery
6 You saw an accident
7 You got sunburned
8 Your freezer broke down
9 You met the Queen
10 You wrote a book
11 You lost your key
12 You were invisible
13 You found a lost dog
14 You found an injured animal
15 Your car broke down on an isolated road
16 You caught the wrong train
17 You got lost on a country walk
18 You had a power cut
19 You discovered a burglary
20 You ran out of milk
21 You found someone lying on the floor
22 You were being followed
23 You were given a plane ticket to go anywhere in the world
24 You were upset by a friend
25 You could shop anywhere you liked
26 You could perform magic
27 You were asked to throw a party
28 You were asked to show someone round where you live
29 You had to organise a takeaway for ten friends
30 You ordered a hamper for Christmas

12 Role Playing

Using speech or mime, members of the group practise situations which they might find difficult to cope with.

1 Ordering flowers over the telephone
2 Answering a wrong-number call
3 Joining a library
4 Finding out times of church services
5 Putting an advertisement in the paper
6 Opening a savings account
7 Dealing with doorstep salespeople
8 Dealing with noisy neighbours
9 Booking a taxi
10 Asking a neighbour to get some shopping
11 Returning an item of clothing to a shop
12 Enrolling for an evening class
13 Being a patient at the dentist's
14 Complaining about a bad meal in a restaurant
15 Asking a pharmacist for advice about an embarrassing medical problem
16 Asking a police officer for directions
17 Asking for a pay rise
18 Posting a parcel
19 Ordering a pizza delivery
20 Talking to a hearing-impaired person
21 Ordering a round of drinks
22 Paying your fare on the bus
23 Choosing a holiday at the travel agent
24 Paying the bill in a restaurant
25 Approaching a stranger at a party
26 Choosing flowers for a present at the florist
27 Making a best man's speech
28 Choosing treatments at a health farm
29 Trying to find out which platform your train goes from
30 Applying for a loan

13 Cook up a Story

The leader starts off a story with one of the phrases below. The first group member finishes the sentence and the next member adds another. Continue for a few sentences until the group runs out of steam. A tape recorder can be used to record the stories and play them back if requested.

1 'The doorbell rang …'
2 'The fire was getting bigger …'
3 'The wind blew my hat off …'
4 'It was peaceful and …'
5 'A wonderful smell came from …'
6 'I was so angry that …'
7 'The film was boring so …'
8 '"What a magnificent view", he said …'
9 'The baby started to cry …'
10 'She was searching for the candles …'
11 'She opened the present and …'
12 'They turned the corner and saw …'
13 'As a treat for my birthday we …'
14 'The plane had just taken off when …'
15 'I was walking the dog when …'
16 'Suddenly, the lights went out …'
17 'Help, cried the man …'
18 'We were feeding the birds when …'
19 'The sun was shining so we …'
20 'The children were excited because …'
21 'The dog was barking because …'
22 'I looked in the mirror and saw …'
23 'In my photo album I found …'
24 'I decided to tidy the house because …'
25 'My holiday this year will be …'
26 'I am going shopping to buy …'

27 'At Christmas, John decided to …'
28 'Susan wanted to buy a pet, so she …'
29 'David wanted to retire from work because …'
30 'Mary decided to move house because …'

14 The Great Debate

For informal discussion, try the following subjects:

1   What should we do about global warming?
2   Should smoking be banned in public places?
3   Who are your favourite comedians, and why?
4   What's the best way of keeping fit?
5   What is your ideal holiday?
6   What would be your desert island disc?
7   Should people wear furs?
8   Is there life on other planets?
9   Do you enjoy DIY?
10 Would you send your children to a boarding school?
11 Is it wrong to hunt animals for sport?
12 Should we bring back capital punishment?
13 Should young mothers work full time?
14 Do we need the monarchy?
15 Should guns be permitted?
16 Should voting be compulsory?
17 What can be done to increase recycling?
18 Where would you take a tourist who came to stay with you?
19 Have standards of education changed?
20 Has the health service got better or worse in the last five years?
21 Which charity do you think is the most worthwhile?
22 How would you tackle the problem of graffiti?
23 Should people go on diets?
24 What would be your ideal picnic?
25 What are the best television programmes, and why?
26 Are prisons too comfortable?
27 What is your ideal meal?
28 Who would you give an award to, and why?
29 Are we a nation of hypochondriacs?
30 What do you think of Christmas?

15 Wacky Ways with Objects

Think of as many uses as you can for the following items. Be as witty and creative as possible.

1 A long scarf
2 An empty toilet roll
3 A glass of water
4 A rotten egg
5 A wire coathanger
6 A clock that doesn't work
7 An empty eggbox
8 An unwanted CD
9 An old pair of tights
10 A rubber glove
11 Old Christmas cards
12 A balloon
13 A spoon
14 Lipstick
15 A sock
16 A pillow
17 An old tyre
18 An empty wine bottle
19 A tree
20 A million pounds
21 A film container
22 A handkerchief
23 A suitcase
24 An elastic band
25 Double cream
26 A flyswat
27 A toothbrush
28 A can of spray paint
29 Yesterday's newspaper
30 An old sink

16 **What Happened Next?**

Make up a very short story (just a few sentences) beginning with the following:

1 The water was beginning to drip through the ceiling …

2 He put the map away; they were definitely lost …

3 Everything was ready for the guests …

4 She turned just in time to see the door slam and lock her in …

5 As the hot air balloon rose, she felt …

6 I looked behind me in the supermarket queue, and who should I see but …

7 I was just about to switch off the TV when …

8 'Can you tell us a bit more about your invention, professor?' the reporter asked …

9 It was so hot that day, we decided to …

10 The judge looked sternly over his spectacles and said …

11 The car was crawling along in a traffic jam …

12 'Are you ready to order now?' the waitress enquired …

13 As the sun set over the palm trees, we decided to …

14 I went into the shop, wondering whether they would have what I wanted …

15 As the train pulled in I scanned the crowd in the station, looking for …

16 She had never expected to see a polar bear strolling down the high street …

17 My computer has broken down yet again, so I …

18 Just as the conductor raised his baton, a voice in the audience cried …

19 The prime minister looked very serious. 'This is a grave crisis we face,' he began …

20 She was sitting with her feet up on the sofa, feeling very relaxed, when suddenly …

17 Gizmos

Name and describe what you would do with the following items. You may use actual objects or photos of them.

1 Pizza cutter
2 Pastry brush
3 Wine cooler
4 Lava lamp
5 Paper shredder
6 Staple remover
7 Eyelash curlers
8 Skewers
9 Cafetière
10 Hole punch
11 Solar light
12 Mending kit
13 Musical instrument
14 Calculator
15 Vacuum cleaner

18 Where or What Is It?

Imagine you are in a familiar or well-known place and then describe what you can see. This can be used as a group guessing game.

1   An airport
2   Disneyland
3   A zoo
4   A tennis court
5   A cable car
6   A library
7   A roundabout
8   A farm
9   A train
10   Stonehenge
11   A country village
12   A fast-food restaurant
13   A car park
14   A pantomime
15   A railway station
16   A garage
17   A recycling bank
18   A department store
19   A launderette
20   A café
21   A bookshop
22   An amusement arcade
23   A ski resort
24   A television studio
25   A garden
26   A police station
27   A petrol station
28   A party
29   The jungle
30   A casino

NON-VERBAL
ACTIVITIES

1 A Piece of the Action

Each person mimes an action pictured or written on a card which is
hidden from the view of the others. The rest of the group must guess
what it is.

1 Making a cup of tea
2 Having a shower
3 Washing up
4 Building a tower of bricks
5 Drying your hair
6 Starting a car
7 Drying dishes
8 Withdrawing money from a cash point
9 Hanging up a picture
10 Tying shoe laces
11 Swimming
12 Boxing
13 Whisking an egg
14 Using a screwdriver
15 Wrapping a parcel
16 Using a tin opener
17 Taking a photograph
18 Washing hands
19 Polishing shoes
20 Buttering bread
21 Pulling a pint
22 Playing a violin
23 Doing up a zip
24 Frying an egg
25 Doing a stand-up comedy act
26 Playing squash
27 Having an eye test
28 Conducting an orchestra
29 Gardening
30 Having a tooth pulled out

2 Blindfolds

One person puts on a blindfold and then everyone else changes seats. When the blindfold is removed the person has to indicate who has moved and where from. Gesture can be used instead of speech if necessary.

3 Do This, Do That

Members of the group throw a ball to one another. Each person catching the ball has to carry out an action, according to their level of ability, called out by the group leader.

1   Close one eye
2   Pretend to put in hair curlers
3   Touch the floor
4   Mime turning a key in a lock
5   Point to the door
6   Stamp your feet
7   Pretend you are gossiping
8   Touch your shoulder then your nose
9   Touch your knee with one finger
10 Wave both hands
11 Pretend you are firing a gun
12 Mime striking a match
13 Click your fingers
14 Whistle
15 Clap your hands
16 Pretend you are fanning yourself
17 Mime blowing up a balloon
18 Show how you would read a paper
19 Demonstrate flying a kite
20 Show how you would watch television using a remote
21 Pretend you are toasting bread
22 Touch your chin
23 Mime playing with a dog
24 Pretend you are playing peek-a-boo
25 Touch your hair
26 Appear not to be interested
27 Have a fit of giggles
28 Fold your arms
29 Show how you would be scary
30 Hiccup

4 Hive of Activity

The group members are shown a collage or a photo containing lots of activities, for example a fairground, shopping mall or beach. Each person has to mime something that is going on, and the others point to that part of the picture where the activity is taking place.

5 Sign for it

The group have to give directions or ask questions by gestures alone, as if they were explaining something to a foreigner.

1 Catch bus 24
2 This is a good restaurant
3 No milk thanks
4 I want a knife
5 Where's the telephone?
6 Give me your coat
7 Don't go that way
8 Where's your ticket?
9 It costs £5
10 Open the window
11 Would you like something to eat?
12 Go to sleep
13 Please wash your hands
14 I'd like to comb my hair
15 Do you take sugar?
16 Do you have a room?
17 Hello
18 I'm not sure, maybe
19 It's upstairs
20 Go straight ahead
21 Yes
22 I'm not happy
23 May I have a drink?
24 Could you take my photo please?
25 After you
26 I'm full up
27 I'm gasping for a drink
28 I'm dying for a cigarette
29 I'm not well
30 I want to sleep

6 Cacophony

Call out one of the following feelings or emotions, and get the group to use their voices, but not words, to convey it. The aim is to get everyone making a sound together.

Happiness
Anger
Fear
Sadness
Surprise
Doubt

7 Draw Your Feelings

Ask each person to draw a feeling. Put all the pictures in a pile and ask each person in turn to pick up a card and guess what the feeling is.

8 Identification

Objects or pictures are given out to the group and the leader asks people to select items according to the attributes read out. (Words in brackets are only examples of suitable objects.)

1 Transparent (glass)
2 Patterned (cloth)
3 Squashy (plasticine)
4 Crackly (cellophane)
5 Spicy (curry powder)
6 Bitter (lemon)
7 Fluffy (powder puff)
8 Curly (spiral keyring)
9 Fizzy (pop)
10 Sticky (honey)
11 Tiny (bead)
12 Spiky (spaghetti server)
13 Sharp (needle)
14 Knobbly (root ginger)
15 Cold (glass of water)
16 Colourful (set of crayons)
17 Female (picture of a woman)
18 Broken (eggshell)
19 Expensive (ring)
20 Recyclable (newspaper)
21 Dirty (used rag)
22 Old (stone)
23 Sweet (sugar)
24 Rusty (nail)
25 Dead (leaf)
26 Poisonous (bleach)
27 Acidic (vinegar)
28 Fragrant (perfume)
29 Crunchy (crisp)
30 Bouncy (ball)

9 Feely Bag

Several objects are put in a pillowcase and each person is asked to feel for a named object. The object may be removed once it has been located.

10 Look and Remember

A number of everyday objects are placed on a tray and the group are allowed to study it for a while. The tray is removed and then brought back with some additional objects on it. People have to pick out the new objects.

11 Make a Face

Show the appropriate facial expression and gestures for the following.

1   Toothache
2   Shock
3   Surprise
4   Sleepiness
5   Fear
6   Earache
7   Embarrassment
8   Boredom
9   Laughter
10 Interest
11 Stomach ache
12 Nervousness
13 Pride
14 Campness
15 Disapproval
16 Stupidity
17 Being lost
18 Impatience
19 Irritation
20 Stiffness
21 Aggression
22 Concern
23 Alertness
24 Itching
25 Liveliness
26 Drunkenness
27 Unconsciousness
28 Shortsightedness
29 Passivity
30 Sore feet

12 Miming Matters

Some of the group are given a picture of an object. They then mime a sketch, incorporating the object. The rest of the group has to guess what the object is.

1 Watering can
2 Television
3 Personal stereo
4 Map
5 Scissors
6 Power drill
7 Computer mouse
8 Padlock
9 Alarm clock
10 Ladder
11 Toothpick
12 Nail file
13 Trainers
14 Paint
15 Medication
16 Tap
17 Fax machine
18 Hammer
19 Ruler
20 Chainsaw
21 Sink plunger
22 Balloon
23 Glove
24 Toilet
25 Lipstick
26 Earring
27 Screwdriver
28 Hairdryer
29 Umbrella
30 Walking stick

13 What's My Line?

Each person is asked to mime an occupation for the rest of the group to guess.

1 Dentist
2 Painter
3 Orchestra conductor
4 Potter
5 Waiter/waitress
6 Baker
7 Bar person
8 Cowboy
9 Mechanic
10 Bank teller
11 Physiotherapist
12 Vet
13 Chef
14 Train driver
15 Secretary
16 Firefighter
17 Nurse
18 Shelf stacker
19 Prison warder
20 Barrister
21 Cellist
22 Pharmacist
23 Actor/actress
24 Vicar
25 Lifeguard
26 Hotel receptionist
27 Trapeze artist
28 Florist
29 Wine taster
30 Footballer

14 Pass it on

Each person in turn is shown an 'action' picture which they mime to the person next to them. The rest of the group keep their eyes closed. Each person is then 'woken up' to pass on the action. The results can be hilarious, especially if the chain of communication goes haywire.

1   Putting on makeup
2   Icing a cake
3   Threading a needle
4   Doing up a bow tie
5   Putting on suntan lotion
6   Playing tennis
7   Loading a dishwasher
8   Shaking and rolling dice
9   Putting on nail varnish
10 Doing a crossword puzzle
11 Eating an apple
12 Cutting paper
13 Brushing hair
14 Picking flowers
15 Giving a sermon
16 Playing snooker
17 Tidying a room
18 Signing a cheque
19 Milking a cow
20 Stroking a dog
21 Paying a bus fare
22 Stargazing
23 Putting out milk bottles
24 Sunbathing
25 Arguing
26 Making sandwiches
27 Using a remote control
28 Tasting wine
29 Hosing a garden
30 Hanging a picture

15 Picture Bingo

Each person has a large card with pictures on (perhaps downloaded from the internet), like the example below. They also have a pile of small cards depicting objects associated with each location on the large card. They have to match all the small cards to the large one.

PARK	LIBRARY	STREET
SWIMMING POOL	RESTAURANT	CHURCH
SUPERMARKET	CINEMA	BANK

Examples of pictures which might appear in the pile (the following list contains three pictures for each item on the bingo card):

 1 Swing
 2 Steeple
 3 Menu
 4 Traffic light
 5 Vicar
 6 Showers
 7 Librarian
 8 Cars
 9 Trolley
10 Bible
11 Screen
12 Bus
13 Tickets
14 Books
15 Locker
16 Checkout
20 Table setting
21 Tree
22 Towel
23 Popcorn
24 Shelves of food
25 Boating lake
26 Person reading a paper
27 Waiter

16 In the Dark

Each person is asked to take a long look at the room and memorise its contents. Then they are blindfolded, or asked to shut their eyes, and asked to point out a specific object or feature.

17 Taste, Touch and Smell

Each person is given a familiar substance to smell, taste or touch with eyes closed. A list of possible examples is given below. With eyes open, they have to pick out the correct substance from all the others.

Taste

1 Mint sweet
2 Banana
3 Grape
4 Marmite
5 Onion
6 Strawberry jam
7 Kiwi fruit
8 Desiccated coconut
9 Apple
10 Anchovy paste

Touch

1 Comb
2 Button
3 Ball of wool
4 Rubber glove
5 Tin foil
6 Bubble wrap
7 Pocket mirror
8 Teabag
9 Computer mouse
10 Nail file

Smell

1 Soap
2 Curry powder
3 Perfume
4 Garlic
5 Cheese
6 Vanilla essence
7 Vinegar
8 Coffee
9 Bread
10 Laundry liquid
11 Shoe polish

18 Pass the Paper

Using a rolled-up newspaper, each person has to mime an action for the others to guess.

1 Conducting an orchestra
2 Police officer using a truncheon
3 Playing cricket
4 Playing tennis
5 Swatting a fly
6 Digging a hole
7 Playing the flute
8 Rolling pastry
9 Fighting a gun battle
10 Using a phone

READING

1 Match the Action

Everyone is given a number of pictures or words (say nine) on a card.
They have to match picture to picture, word to picture or word to word,
as these are shown or laid out one at a time by the group leader.

1   Praying
2   Waving
3   Bowling
4   Catching
5   Knitting
6   Spreading
7   Typing
8   Dusting
9   Washing
10 Peeling
11 Skipping
12 Shopping
13 Skateboarding
14 Prancing
15 Parachuting
16 Diving
17 Building
18 Pushing
19 Sculpting
20 Harvesting
21 Pulling
22 Flicking
23 Dressing
24 Twisting
25 Punching
26 Joining
27 Beating
28 Driving
29 Drilling
30 Cycling

2 The Advertising Game

Advertisements are pasted onto card and the name of the product is cut off. The cards are shared out among the group and the names are put in a bag for people to select when it is their turn. The advertisement then has to be matched to the name of the product.

3 Sports Bingo

Each person has a big card like the one shown here, and a pile of small cards bearing the words in the list below. The small cards have to be placed in the box to the right of the sport to which they relate. If you want to introduce an element of competition, the person who finishes first and gets the answers right wins the game.

TENNIS		GOLF		SNOOKER	
CRICKET		SWIMMING		BOXING	
FOOTBALL		MOTOR RACING		SKIING	

1	Line judge	**10**	Tee	**20**	White
2	Manchester United	**11**	Ropes	**21**	Sticks
		12	Penalty shootout	**22**	Piste
3	Bails	**13**	Chequered flag	**23**	Pool
4	Wimbledon	**14**	Caddy	**24**	Four-iron
5	Track	**15**	Silly mid off	**25**	Pink
6	Red	**16**	Skis	**26**	Car
7	Crease	**17**	Punchbag	**27**	Yellow card
8	Ring	**18**	Trunks		
9	Diving board	**19**	Racquet		

4 Room Bingo

Each person has a big card like the one shown here, and a pile of small cards bearing the words in the list below. The small cards have to be placed in the box to the right of the room in which they belong. If you want to introduce an element of competition, the person who finishes first and gets the answers right wins the game.

GARAGE		OFFICE		BATHROOM	
BEDROOM		LIVING ROOM		KITCHEN	
DINING ROOM		HALL		GARDEN	

1	Dining table	**10**	Letterbox	**19**	Oven
2	Car	**11**	Oil can	**20**	Armchair
3	Path	**12**	Computer	**21**	Doormat
4	Coat stand	**13**	Bed	**22**	Pond
5	Sofa	**14**	Coffee table	**23**	Shed
6	Cooker	**15**	Desk	**24**	Napkins
7	Shower	**16**	Toilet	**25**	Tyre
8	Wardrobe	**17**	Bath	**26**	Tablecloth
9	Filing cabinet	**18**	Chest of drawers	**27**	Sink

5 Board Game

Preparation

Use a large sheet of card or hardboard to make a board like the one shown here.

START			Have an extra go				Take a card
Take a card			Miss a go				Take a card

The following items are also needed:

Small cards
Die
Counters

Write questions appropriate to the ability of the group on the cards and place these in a pile in the centre of the board.

How to play

1   Each person takes a turn to shake the die and then moves their counter accordingly.
2   They have to follow any instructions written on the square they land on.
3   Finally, they pick up a card from the centre of the board and answer the written question. If they get the question right they keep the card. When all the cards have been used up, the person with the most cards is the winner.

6 Comprehension Passages

Newspaper articles, magazine clippings, etc of different lengths, themes and complexity can be used for the group to read and answer questions on. The questions may be verbal or written.

7 Desert Island Discs

Present a list of tunes that you have access to, and ask everyone to vote for their three favourites to take to a desert island. Play these during the coffee breaks or at some suitable time.

8 Double Name Game

Two words that go together are written on cards, one in red ink, the other in green. The red cards are shared out equally among the group. The green ones are placed in the centre of the table for each person in turn to pick up and read out the word. The word has to be paired with a red card belonging to someone in the group.

	Red	Green		Red	Green
1	Remote	control	16	Hockey	stick
2	Sun	glasses	17	Curtain	rail
3	Tooth	pick	18	Net	ball
4	Sausage	roll	19	Bean	bag
5	Place	mat	20	Answering	machine
6	Pencil	sharpener	21	Paper	clip
7	Tea	strainer	22	Bus	stop
8	Washer	dryer	23	Personal	stereo
9	CD	player	24	Garlic	crusher
10	Green	house	25	Ice-cream	maker
11	Cork	screw	26	Dustbin	lid
12	Compact	disc	27	Cough	mixture
13	Can	opener	28	Lemon	sorbet
14	Dressing	gown	29	Light	bulb
15	Cricket	bat	30	Picture	frame

9 Hitting the Headlines

Each person has a sheet from a newspaper, and the group leader reads out a headline from another copy of the paper for the rest of the group to find as quickly as possible.

10 Read the Label

Cut out the lists of ingredients from food packaging and paste them onto cards. Write down the names of the foods on another set of cards, and ask participants to match the two.

11 Odd One Out

A whiteboard or paper can be used for this game. The idea is to underline the word which does not go with the other two.

1   House – bungalow – car
2   Lion – robin – zebra
3   Merry – jolly – long
4   Seagull – sparrow – seat
5   Infant – child – nurse
6   Circle – box – rectangle
7   Jumping – sleeping – leaping
8   Knife – scissors – corkscrew
9   Sock – shoe – hat
10 Narrow – skipping – slender
11 Table – fax – telephone
12 Fish – bicycle – car
13 Paper – cardboard – ant
14 Chair – rain – snow
15 Kite – music – orchestra
16 Kevin – Sharon – Charlotte
17 Blue – black – round
18 Hat – apple – pear
19 Soap – oven – hob
20 Cat – dog – motorway
21 Book – pimple – magazine
22 Brick – donkey – concrete
23 Theatre – telescope – cinema
24 Mountain – happy – angry
25 Keyboard – mouse – cushion
26 Rose – luggage – daisy
27 Sink – lips – nose
28 Window – horse – door
29 Heart – lung – clock
30 Wall – purse – bag

12 Cheesy Rhymes

Cut six circles of paper or card by drawing round a dinner plate. Divide each one into six equal segments by drawing straight lines across it to make the shape of a cut cheese. Take one of the circles, and in each segment, write one of the following words:

CAN

YOU

MAKE

CHEESE

EACH

WEEK

Now cut the remaining five circles into segments and write the following words on the segments:

Van	Shoe	Take
Span	Zoo	Bake
Tan	Too	Shake
Fan	Clue	Rake
Superman	Hullabaloo	Rattlesnake
Bees	Peach	Peak
Sneeze	Teach	Speak
Tease	Beach	Meek
Fees	Preach	Tweak
Pekinese	Overreach	Mozambique

Shuffle the segments and distribute them equally to group members. Each person has to place their segments on the relevant areas of the cheese.

13 Highway Code

Obtain a copy of the Highway Code and paste the pictures of road signs on to cards. Write out what the signs mean on another set of cards. Participants have to match the two sets of cards.

14 Names to Faces

Cut out photos of famous people from magazines. Write their names on cards or a sheet of paper and get participants to match the names to the faces. Encourage any discussion that might follow.

15 Summing Up

1 People are given passages to read, perhaps cut out of newspapers or magazines, with a choice of summaries at the end. They have to select the one which describes the passage they have just read.

Example

My daughter sent me a postcard yesterday. She is on holiday in Spain for two weeks. She says that the weather is hot and sunny and that she is getting very tanned. The people are friendly and the hotel is well placed for the beach. She seems to be enjoying herself and is not looking forward to returning home.

(i) The daughter is having a good holiday.

(ii) She is hoping to live in Spain.

(iii) She is working in a Spanish hotel.

2 The same may be done with sentences with a choice of key words at the end to describe the essence of the sentence.

Example

I had to go out and buy lots of food for the kitchen cupboard.

(i) gardening

(ii) shopping

(iii) washing up

16 What Am I?

Using PowerPoint write out the following descriptions, one to each slide. Get people to shout out the answer to each one. There may be more than one answer to each question.

1 I am used to sweeten food (sugar)
2 I am electrical and clean the carpet (vacuum cleaner)
3 I am electrical and dry your hair (hairdryer)
4 I have a lens and take your photograph (camera)
5 I am sliced to make toast (bread)
6 I am slept on (bed)
7 I am a bird eaten on Christmas Day (turkey)
8 I bring your food to the table in a restaurant (waiter/waitress)
9 I design buildings (architect)
10 I stand in front of an orchestra and wave a baton (conductor)
11 I stand up in church and give sermons (vicar)
12 I am used to time races (stopwatch)
13 I have a crystal ball and can tell your future (fortune teller)
14 I have a trigger and fire bullets (gun)
15 I break in and steal your things (burglar)
16 I am smeared all over your body to protect you from the sun (sunscreen)
17 I help you read and write (teacher)
18 I have rungs (ladder)
19 I have a grassbox (lawnmower)
20 I book your holidays (travel agent)
21 I am used to scrub your back in the bath (backbrush)
22 I ring to make you get up in the morning (alarm clock)
23 I am a musical instrument that is sometimes known as a fiddle (violin)
24 I am a car that carries coffins (hearse)
25 I am the capital of Italy (Rome)
26 I tape television programmes when you are out (video)
27 I am the most common piece in a chess game (pawn)
28 I live in water and end up in a cocktail (prawn)
29 I run the country (prime minister)
30 I decide what goes on the front page of a newspaper (editor)

17 Country Bingo

Each person has a big card like the one shown here, and a pile of shuffled small cards bearing the words in the list opposite. The small cards have to be placed in the box to the right of the country in which they belong. If you want to introduce an element of competition, the person who finishes first and gets the answers right wins the game.

FRANCE		AUSTRALIA		GREECE	
SPAIN		USA		CHINA	
GERMANY		ITALY		JAPAN	

The cards should be shuffled before they are handed out.

Eiffel Tower	Sydney	Acropolis
Foie Gras	Aborigines	Corfu
EuroDisney	Kangaroos	Athens
Côte d'Azur	Boomerangs	Retsina
St Tropez	Fosters	The Onassis Family
Barcelona	Hollywood	The Great Wall
Madrid	Miami	Shanghai
Costa del Sol	Baseball	Dim Sum
Bullfights	Wall Street	Chairman Mao
Tapas	Cheerleaders	Beijing
Berlin	Florence	Kimono
Frankfurt	Gondolas	Karaoke
Black Forest	Sicily	Tea Ceremonies
Volkswagen	The Mafia	Tokyo
Sauerkraut	Armani	Sushi

18 Chain Letters

A flipchart or whiteboard is useful for this game. People take turns to write a word beginning with the last letter of the previous word. To make this more difficult, the words might be related to a particular theme, for example food or clothes.

WRITING

1 A Day in the Life

Each group member is given a picture of a person, either cut out from a magazine or downloaded from the internet. They are asked to write a short piece describing a day in that person's life.

2 Free Association

Write down as many words as possible that are associated with each of the following:

1 Water
2 Sand
3 Garden
4 Wine
5 Fun
6 Boredom
7 Travel
8 Relaxation
9 Treasure
10 Countryside
11 Dinner
12 Snake
13 Tiny
14 Queen
15 Police
16 Religion
17 Station
18 Milk
19 Eyes
20 Book
21 Cat
22 Christmas
23 Hospital
24 Ireland
25 Island
26 Camera
27 Vegetable
28 Desert
29 Ice-cream
30 Summer

3 Top Twenty

Write down your favourite of each of the following:

1 Flower
2 Zoo animal
3 Car
4 Holiday
5 Film star
6 Pet
7 Gadget
8 Place in this country
9 Colour
10 Politician
11 Television programme
12 Meal
13 Hobby
14 Shop
15 Musician
16 Book
17 Member of the royal family
18 Word
19 Smell
20 Household task

4 Book codes

Divide the group into pairs and give each pair a book. The first member of the pair makes up a sentence, using words taken from the book. For each word, they write down the page number on which it occurs, the line number and the number of the word in that line. The second person then has to reconstruct the sentence.

5 Scrambled Songs

Unscramble the following:

1 out roll barrel the
2 hard it's night been a day's
3 to heaven stairway
4 things beautiful bright all and
5 jolly a for good he's fellow
6 to birthday happy you
7 around rock clock the
8 rain the in singing
9 over somewhere rainbow the
10 faithful come O ye all
11 lonesome you are tonight
12 brick yellow road goodbye
13 the sheriff shot I
14 all save kisses your me for
15 head raindrops falling keep on my
16 the Jose way do know you to San
17 ivy holly and the the
18 the wind in candle
19 Christmas know they it's do
20 never alone you'll walk
21 dance music let's the face and
22 goodbye we every say time
23 up Susie little wake
24 of lord hopefulness all
25 David's once city in royal
26 grass the of green home green
27 old my man's dustman a
28 cliffs white the of Dover
29 no I can't satisfaction get
30 MacDonald farm had old a

6 Jumblies

The group are given anagrams related to a particular theme to solve.
Examples:

1 Colours
2 Film stars
3 Members of the royal family
4 Politicians
5 Body parts
6 Areas of your town or city
7 Makeup
8 Medicines
9 Supermarkets
10 Clothes shops
11 Cocktails
12 Alcoholic drinks
13 Soft drinks
14 First aid items
15 Soft furnishings
16 Household goods
17 Boys' names
18 Girls' names
19 Emotions
20 Occupations
21 Footwear
22 Newspapers
23 Musicals
24 Holiday destinations
25 Fashion accessories
26 Road signs
27 Sections of a supermarket
28 Stationery
29 Kitchenware
30 Capital cities

7 Pasty Faces

Interesting faces from magazines are pasted onto card and given to the group to write about.

8 You're the Chef

The names of recipes are given and the group has to write down possible ingredients.

Examples
1 Pancake
2 Fish pie
3 Vegetable soup
4 Jam tarts
5 Fruit cake
6 Ratatouille
7 Marmalade
8 Apple crumble
9 Porridge
10 Pesto sauce

9 Same and Different

For each of these words, there are others that sound the same but are spelled differently. The group is shown a list of words, and they have to write down one word which sounds the same. They then have to put each pair of words into a meaningful sentence. For example, the first sentence might be 'I know of no reason'. The words in brackets may not be the only answers.

1	Know	*(No)*		16	Pore	*(Pour)*
2	Bore	*(Boar)*		17	Dye	*(Die)*
3	Side	*(Sighed)*		18	World	*(Whirled)*
4	Teas	*(Tease)*		19	Carrot	*(Carat)*
5	Wail	*(Whale)*		20	Waist	*(Waste)*
6	Bare	*(Bear)*		21	Pete	*(Peat)*
7	Alter	*(Altar)*		22	Adds	*(Ads)*
8	Ball	*(Bawl)*		23	Fir	*(Fur)*
9	Seek	*(Sikh)*		24	Allowed	*(Aloud)*
10	Cell	*(Sell)*		25	Find	*(Fined)*
11	Sighs	*(Size)*		26	Heal	*(Heel)*
12	Witch	*(Which)*		27	Knead	*(Need)*
13	Shoe	*(Shoo)*		28	Meet	*(Meat)*
14	Dear	*(Deer)*		29	Road	*(Rowed)*
15	Quay	*(Key)*		30	Sale	*(Sail)*

10 Storyline

Write a story containing as many as possible of the following words.

1 Entertain
2 Grab
3 Mystery
4 Ankle
5 Punch
6 Rabbit
7 Slice
8 Zookeeper
9 Travel
10 Tunnel
11 Young
12 Australia
13 Happy
14 Expensive
15 Weird

11 The Noun Game

Put each of these nouns into a sentence.

1   Ginger
2   Dustbin
3   Lavender
4   Diary
5   Microwave
6   Office
7   Book
8   Hooligan
9   House
10 Darkness
11 Baby
12 Burglar
13 Monster
14 Launderette
15 Bath
16 Model
17 Gunpowder
18 Holiday
19 Song
20 Wedding
21 Perfume
22 Ghost
23 Train
24 Weather
25 Apron
26 Dream
27 Garden
28 Bottle
29 Doctor
30 Television

12 The Adjective Game

Put each of these adjectives into a sentence.

1   Slight
2   Interesting
3   Rapid
4   Greedy
5   Intelligent
6   Blue
7   Active
8   Attractive
9   Drunk
10 Foreign
11 Huge
12 Bumpy
13 Slim
14 Square
15 Irritable
16 Correct
17 Imaginary
18 Difficult
19 Embarrassing
20 Cold
21 Sleepy
22 Exciting
23 Sharp
24 Cheerful
25 Funny
26 Unusual
27 Dead
28 Circular
29 Slippery
30 Hot

13 Millionaire

You've won a million pounds. Write a few words or sentences describing what you would do with it, and share this with the group. Alternatively, the leader reads out the responses and members have to guess who wrote them.

14 Dream Holiday

Write down your idea of a dream holiday. How would you travel, what would you wear, where would you stay, what would you eat, drink, do and see? Share responses with the rest of the group. Alternatively, the leader reads out the answers and members have to guess who wrote them.

15 Heaven on Earth

Imagine you are looking for the perfect place to live. Tell the estate
agent the location, style of property, décor and facilities it should have.
Describe the perfect neighbours and what the garden should be like.

16 Letting off Steam

Come up with a list of your ten pet hates and read them out to the
group. You may want to disguise who wrote the responses and ask
people to guess who the pet hate belongs to.

17 Secret Santa

Your family have decided to put everyone's name on a piece of paper in a hat, and you pull out a name and have to buy a present costing £10. Write down who you would choose and a list of possible gifts costing as close to £10 as possible. The leader might set a time limit on the activity or ask each person to come up with three or more ideas.

All the gifts could be put into one list and members vote for their favourite present.

Writing

18 Postbag

Write a letter for one of the purposes listed here.

1. A competition entry on why you should win a holiday for two in Spain.
2. How an airline could improve their inflight service.
3. Describe a birthday surprise to a friend.
4. Offer to housesit for a friend and explain what jobs you would do.
5. Congratulate a couple getting married, giving them advice on how to stay happy.
6. Tell your local member of Parliament how your local area could be improved.
7. Design your own birthday card and write a message.
8. Send a household tip to a magazine's letters page.
9. Write a wedding invitation and provide a presents list.
10. Send advice to a magazine aimed at the elderly, on how to enjoy retirement.